Our Universe

The Sun

by Margaret J. Goldstein

Lerner Publications Company • Minneapolis

Lerner Publications Company
A division of Lerner Publishing Group
241 First Avenue North
Minneapolis, MN 55401 USA

Website address: www.lernerbooks.com

Words in **bold type** are explained in a glossary on page 30.

Library of Congress Cataloging-in-Publication Data

Goldstein, Margaret J.
        The sun / by Margaret J. Goldstein.
            p.   cm. – (Our universe)
        Includes index.
        Summary: An introduction to the Sun and the planets
    that make up the solar system.
        ISBN: 0–8225–4647–7 (lib. bdg. : alk. paper)
        1. Sun—Juvenile literature. 2. Solar system—Juvenile
    literature. [1. Sun. 2. Solar system. 3. Planets.] I. Title.
    II. Series.
        QB521.5 .G65 2003
        523.2–dc21   2002006838

Manufactured in the United States of America
1 2 3 4 5 6 – JR – 08 07 06 05 04 03

You can see thousands of stars on a clear night. But only one star can be seen during the day. It lights up our sky. What is this star?

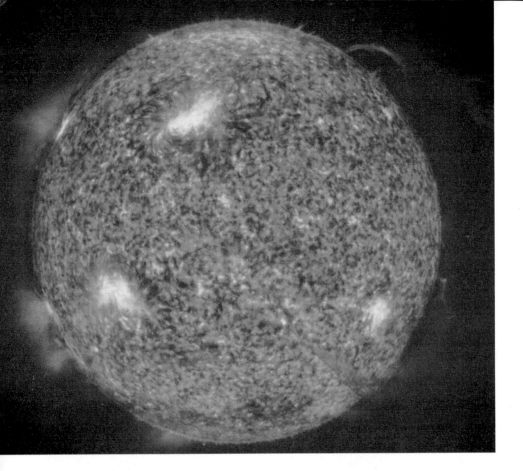

This star is the Sun. The Sun is the closest star to Earth. Earth is our home planet.

The Sun is at the center of the **solar system.** The solar system has nine planets in all. Earth is one of the nine planets.

All of the planets in the solar system travel around the Sun. Earth is the third planet from the sun.

THE SOLAR SYSTEM

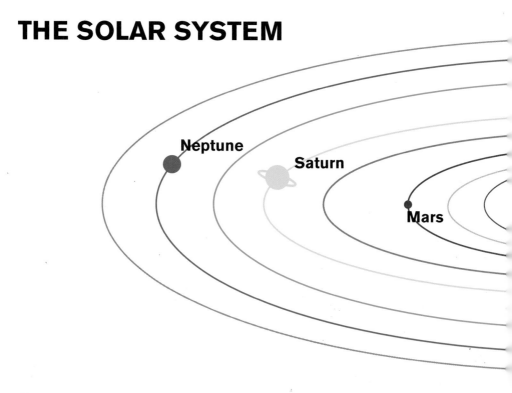

The Sun's heat and light travel out to the planets in the solar system. The planets close to the Sun get the most heat and light. Planets far from the Sun get much less heat and light.

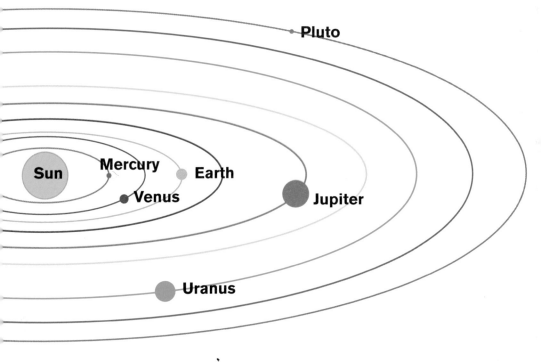

The Sun is much bigger than anything else in the solar system. More than a million planets like Earth could fit inside the Sun. But the Sun is not the biggest or brightest star in space.

The Sun

Earth

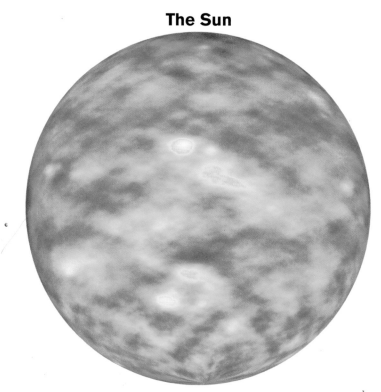

The Sun is a medium-sized star. But it is the closest star to Earth. So it looks bigger and brighter than other stars. Other stars look small because they are very far away.

Like all stars, the Sun is a giant ball of hot gases. It is like a huge furnace. Temperatures deep inside the Sun are millions of degrees above zero. That is much, much hotter than any place on Earth.

The inside of the Sun is called the **core.** Heat from the core travels to the outside of the Sun. The outside of the Sun is called the **surface.** The surface is not as hot as the core. But it is still very hot.

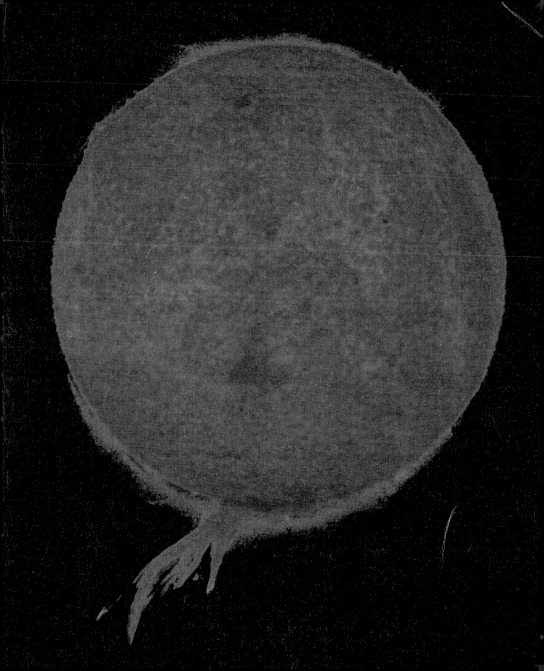

Some places on the surface of the Sun are cooler than other places. These cooler places are called **sunspots.** Sunspots look like small dark patches on the Sun.

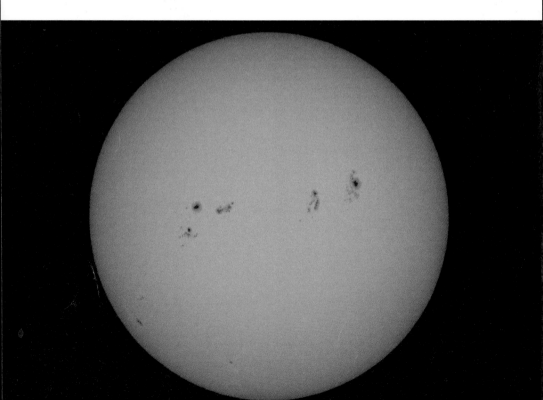

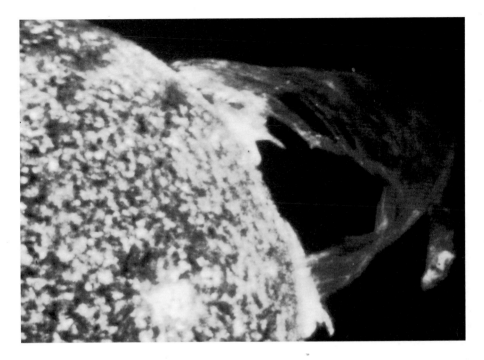

Sometimes glowing gases shoot up
from the surface of the Sun. The gases
make big loops. The Sun also gives off
bursts of light and heat. The bursts are
called **solar flares.**

Streams of tiny **particles** flow from the Sun. These particles are called the **solar wind**. Blasts of the solar wind sometimes reach Earth.

You cannot see or feel the solar wind. But it can cause the sky on Earth to glow at night. This glowing light is called an **aurora.** Auroras happen only in the far northern and southern parts of Earth.

The Sun lights up our sky during the day. The Sun seems to rise in the sky in the morning and sink again at night. The Sun looks like it is moving because Earth is always spinning.

DAY AND NIGHT

Earth's spinning

Earth spins like a top. The spinning gives us day and night. In the morning, your side of Earth spins to face the Sun. In the evening, your side of Earth spins back away from the Sun.

Sometimes the Moon seems to cover up the Sun. The Moon circles Earth. As the Moon travels, it sometimes moves between Earth and the Sun. Then the Moon blocks the Sun's light for a few minutes. On parts of Earth, the sky grows dark. This event is called a **solar eclipse.**

The Sun is very important to Earth. The Sun warms the land and the oceans on our planet. Sunlight helps keep people, plants, and animals warm, too.

Sunlight also helps plants grow. People and animals need plants for food. Without the Sun, there would be no food to eat. There would be no life on Earth.

Humans have wondered about the Sun for thousands of years. But people cannot look right at the Sun for very long. The Sun's bright light is too strong.

Astronomers are people who study outer space. Astronomers use special telescopes to look at the Sun. These telescopes help astronomers study the Sun without harming their eyes.

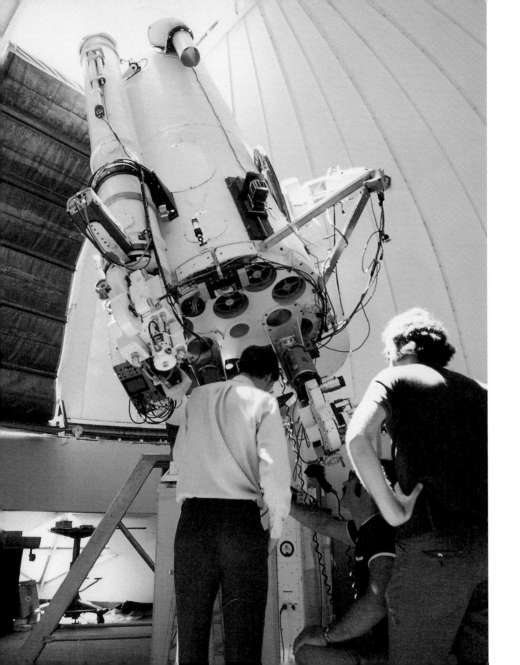

Astronauts have studied the Sun. Astronauts are people who travel from Earth to space. In the 1970s, astronauts studied the Sun from a space station called *Skylab.*

Spacecraft without astronauts have studied the Sun, too. The spacecraft carried machines that measured the Sun's heat and light. They also carried cameras that took pictures of the Sun.

An artist made this picture of a spacecraft visiting the Sun.

A spacecraft called *Genesis* left Earth in 2001. It is traveling toward the Sun. *Genesis* will study the solar wind. It will collect particles from the solar wind and bring them back to Earth.

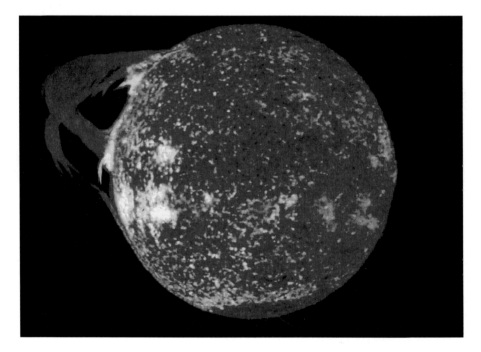

You can see the Sun shine. You can feel its heat on your skin. Ask your own questions about the Sun. Then try to find the answers.

Facts about the Sun

- The Sun is about 93,000,000 miles (150,000,000 km) from Earth.

- The Sun is 36,000,000 miles (58,000,000 km) from Mercury, the innermost planet in the solar system, and 3,666,000,000 miles (5,900,100,00 km) from Pluto, the outermost planet.

- The Sun's diameter (distance across) is 864,000 miles (1,400,000 km).

- The average temperature of the Sun's core is 27,000,000°F (15,000,000°C).

- The average temperature of the Sun's surface is 10,000°F (5,500°C).

- The Sun is made mostly of hydrogen and helium, but at least 70 other gases also are part of the Sun.

- Some stars are 1,000 times wider than the Sun.

- The Sun is at least 4.5 billion years old.

- The Sun is brighter than all the lightbulbs on Earth put together.

- The Sun will keep shining for about another 5 billion years.

- The Sun is much too hot for any person to stand on it. A human would burn up long before reaching the Sun.

- The Sun has strong gravity, the force that pulls you toward the ground. If you weighed 80 pounds on Earth, you would weigh 2,244 pounds on the Sun!

- At least one dozen spacecraft are studying the Sun or the effects of the Sun on Earth.

Glossary

astronauts: people who travel to outer space

astronomers: people who study outer space

aurora: colored lights that glow in the sky in far northern and southern parts of Earth

core: the center of the Sun

particles: tiny bits of matter

solar eclipse: when the Moon blocks out the Sun's light

solar flares: bursts of heat and light that shoot up from the Sun

solar system: the Sun and the planets, moons, and other objects that travel around it

solar wind: tiny particles that flow from the Sun

surface: the outer layer of an object

sunspots: dark patches on the Sun's surface

Learn More about the Sun

Books

Furniss, Tim. *The Sun.* Austin, TX: Raintree Steck-Vaughn, 2000.

Lassieur, Allison. *The Sun.* New York: Children's Press, 2000.

Websites

Solar System Exploration: The Sun
<http://solarsystem.nasa.gov/features/planets/sun/sun.html>
Detailed information from the National Aeronautics and Space
Administration (NASA) about the Sun, with good links to other
helpful websites.

The Space Place
<http://spaceplace.jpl.nasa.gov>
An astronomy website for kids developed by NASA's Jet
Propulsion Laboratory.

StarChild
<http://starchild.gsfc.nasa.gov/docs/StarChild/StarChild.html>
An online learning center for young astronomers, sponsored by
NASA.

Index